Heart and Soul

OUR BEAUTIFUL LOVE STORY IN POETRY

Written by Bea Boxx

With Poetry by John Boxx

WestBow Press books may be ordered through booksellers or by contacting:

WestBow Press
A Division of Thomas Nelson & Zondervan
1663 Liberty Drive
Bloomington, IN 47403
www.westbowpress.com
1 (866) 928-1240

Because of the dynamic nature of the Internet, any web addresses or links contained in this book may have changed since publication and may no longer be valid. The views expressed in this work are solely those of the author and do not necessarily reflect the views of the publisher, and the publisher hereby disclaims any responsibility for them.

Any people depicted in stock imagery provided by Thinkstock are models, and such images are being used for illustrative purposes only.
Certain stock imagery © Thinkstock.

ISBN: 978-1-5127-3510-9 (sc)
ISBN: 978-1-5127-3511-6 (e)

Library of Congress Control Number: 2016904408

Print information available on the last page.

WestBow Press rev. date: 03/28/2016

WESTBOW
P R E S S®
A DIVISION OF THOMAS NELSON
& ZONDERVAN

CONTENTS

FOREWORD

By Bailey Foster, Writer & Editor, Penned Precision, LLC

When I agreed to review and edit this book, I didn't anticipate the depth of emotion I would encounter within its pages. What began as an intriguing professional project quickly grew into something more significant. Through my work on *Heart and Soul*, I have been reminded of truths easily taken for granted, life lessons easily forgotten, and a kind of love *not* so easily sustained.

It has been a true privilege to share in the completion of this book – a story that beautifully honors the love shared by John and Bea Boxx. Striking in its simplicity, moving in its message, and profound in its purpose, *Heart and Soul* prompts in the reader an immediate sense of awe over John and Bea's unmistakable love for one another, which then develops into a greater feeling of admiration and inspiration.

The love reflected within the poems and narratives of this book captures the essence of human romance – romance in all its enchantment and passion. And yet what makes this love truly distinct is its transcendence of pervasive social and cultural definitions. To John and Bea, love was more than a fleeting emotion. It was an ongoing commitment to intentionally *live* their wedding vows, undeterred by trials, fears, and uncertainties. It was a day-in, day-out exercise in selflessness, appreciation, and devotion. It was a love that's not often attained in our culture of quick fixes and habitual conveniences – but one that's well worth the dedication and effort required to nurture it.

Over the course of my work on *Heart and Soul*, I have learned so much from John and Bea about what it means to live and love without fear. In a world that's not always kind, it's tempting to let difficulties consume us. Yet when we choose to move boldly, love relentlessly, and look for beauty in unexpected places, we see that life consists of countless fragments - some jagged, some smooth, but all meaningful. John and Bea show us that contentment lies in appreciating what we have, in cherishing seemingly insignificant moments, and in realizing that time is precious and short.

In contrast to the superficial images of love all around us, this book provides an honest picture of what love *should* look like – giving oneself joyfully and selflessly to another and choosing to love in spite of the circumstances. As you read the pages that follow and share in the heart-grasping story of two wonderful people, may you be inspired to love with intention and determination, and in doing so, pass on the poignant message of *Heart and Soul.*

For the love of my life

ACKNOWLEDGEMENTS

My deepest thanks to those who have helped me accomplish my dream to publish John's beautiful poetry and to share our story.

Beth, Stacey, Jeff, and Maryann gave me encouragement and advice throughout the project, especially when doubt crept in. Bailey from Penned Precision, LLC added an extra special, professional touch to communicate the overall purpose and inspiration for the memoir.

The poetry expresses our undying love for each other and was written from John's heart and soul. The photos paired with the poetry represent some of our treasured memories we made together. They capture the beauty we experienced in places near, in places far and all around us. They offer depictions of love and relationships that are both personal and symbolic.

PROLOGUE

"At the touch of love, everyone becomes a poet."
~Plato

We never know when true love will take hold of us. Perhaps that's part of its beauty and mystery – what makes it so precious and all-consuming. Once we have it, we never want to let it go.

The day that love found me is a permanent, vivid part of my memory – when I first sat across from the man who would be my husband for 19 beautiful years. The man who would embody my girlhood dreams of a Prince Charming, a knight in shining armor, a forever love, a soul mate. The man who would bring poetry to my life, poetry that's forever etched upon my heart and being.

It was 1993, and my company had transferred me from Atlanta to Tampa. Destiny smiled on this seemingly insignificant career transition, inconspicuously guiding me to the love of my life. Several managers, mentors, and guardian angels lined up our meant-to-be-moment.

I remember the day like it was yesterday. I sat in John's office with my savvy account manager and mentor, smelling Obsession from across the room, his favorite cologne. John was smart, sharp, quick-witted, driven, confident – and gorgeous. The attraction between us was immediate and mutual.

My firm had been selected to partner with John's company on an exciting pilot project. Despite my short tenure, I was privileged to work as an in-house analyst on the project – yet another twist of fate in our developing love story. For the next eighteen months, I worked side-by-side with John.

We quickly became an incredible team, yet were unconscious of the deep personal bond that was forming. Our daily interactions as colleagues planted the seeds of our beautiful friendship, which then blossomed unexpectedly into a life-long attraction.

As my eighteenth month on the project drew near, I felt anxiety and sadness begin to grow in my heart. On my last day on-site, I stopped by John's office for one last good-bye. Neither of us anticipated the emotions that welled up. As I turned to leave his office, John jumped up out of his chair, grabbed me, and held me close – like he was afraid I would be gone forever. I dashed out of the building so fast and let the tears flow, feeling like Cinderella leaving the ball at midnight. My magical time was over; I couldn't envision a future with my Prince Charming.

As it turned out, we were both wrong. Several very long months passed with no contact between us. Then, my company reorganized, and I was promoted to account manager. My new account – John's company! Once again, we would work together and see each other regularly. To say we were both thrilled was an understatement. And after a time apart, the magnetism between us only grew stronger.

The poetry and love notes started eight months before we married. John would leave me voice messages echoing his feelings of love. As I listened, I put every word on paper, filling my journal with his notes and poems.

As the little girl who had always believed in fairy tales, I had finally met a man who mesmerized me, a man who sent me love notes and proclaimed his love in voice messages filled with poetry. He was everything I had ever dreamed about. I was whole-heartedly, completely, head-over-heels in love.

John was a hopeless romantic which I cherished. When he found out I was born in Key West but had never been back, he vowed to take me himself and marry me there. On our first trip to Key West, John bought our wedding bands. And although we eloped in August of 1996 while picking up our marriage licenses, John kept his promise and took me back to Key West for a private wedding ceremony. On September 9, 1996, we exchanged rings in a beautiful, tropical garden in the middle of the island.

The story of our love is not one marked by fame or notoriety. It's a story of two ordinary people who shared an extraordinary bond. A marriage bursting with friendship, companionship, passion, and total devotion to each other. An amazing blessing from

God. Through the poems and thoughts that follow, we seek to tell this story and share our beautiful life of love.

In a book that John gave to me called "True Love," there is a quote that says, "True Love increases as you give it away." My hope and John's enduring wish, is to share our gift of love and our beautiful marriage with the world, inspiring you to chase dreams, pursue meaningful relationships, and love fearlessly - with heart and soul.

PART 1 · TWO HEARTS MADE ONE

"Whatever our souls are made of, his and mine are the same."
~*Emily Bronte,* Wuthering Heights

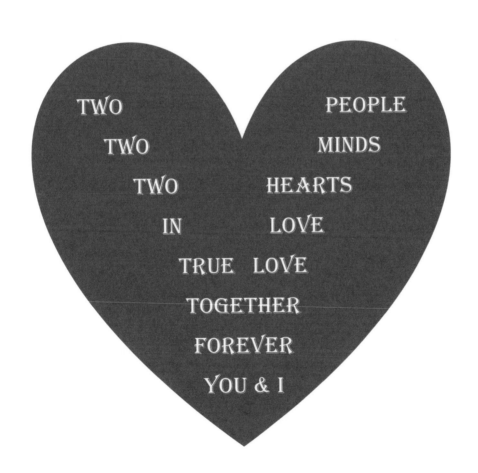

TWO   PEOPLE

TWO   MINDS

TWO   HEARTS

IN   LOVE

TRUE LOVE

TOGETHER

FOREVER

YOU & I

BEHIND THE POEM – MY PRECIOUS FLOWER

"For it was not into my ear you whispered but into my heart. It was not my lips that you kissed, but my soul."
~Judy Garland

John invited me to lunch for the first Valentine's Day since we had known each other. As work colleagues, we knew we shouldn't, but neither one of us was willing to stop what seemed destined. He had spaghetti and meatballs, and I had chicken parmesan, a lunch we would share many times over the years. I still have my first Valentine gifts from him: the card, the coffee mug that says "Today, Tomorrow, Forever, I Love You," and the little cow that plays a lullaby.

After lunch, we both went back to our respective offices. I wasn't very focused the rest of the day and worked quietly in my little cubicle. Around 4:00 p.m., I received a call from the region manager's assistant. She told me I had a delivery. I walked to her desk, and she gave me a small vase with two long-stemmed red roses and a card attached with a ribbon. The message on the card was a simple rhyme:

'Cause I thought of just a single rose,
But alas that would not do.
For one is so you'll think of me;
The other is to say "I love you."

There was no name, but I knew immediately they were from John.

Soon after the roses arrived, John called me and was insistent that I meet him that evening for just a short while. Under a streetlight, he pulled out several hand-written pages. On the pages was a poem he had written, and he read it to me as I fought back tears. After reading "**My Precious Flower,**" he looked into my eyes and said, "I am smitten with you." He told me he wanted to marry me. We hugged and kissed, and of course I cried.

The first touch of love is a memory that stays with us. The intense mingling of emotions, from fear and doubt to exhilaration and pure joy, is not easily forgotten.

John's words in **"My Precious Flower"** give beautiful insight into his earliest feelings of love for me, feelings that only grew and became more meaningful with time. The magnolia photos that accompany John's words were taken in our garden. The white magnolia represents beauty, perfection, and things at their beginning - a perfect complement to start our beautiful love story.

MY PRECIOUS FLOWER

I saw one day, a blossom, small, petite, demure.
It captured my attention with some sweet, secret allure.

I looked away quickly fearing the stir inside,
Not understanding the emotion and seeking just to hide.

Surely this blossom would never notice me,
For when it became a flower, a thing of beauty it would be.

I watched in great amazement as each day its beauty grew,
As petals slowly unfurled, sweet and soft and true.

I once again retreated to hide so not to see,
For surely this thing of beauty would never notice me.

But as this flower blossomed, a glow began to form
That showered over me so beautiful and warm.

I reached out to touch it and hold it in my hand.
I was filled with unknown feelings that I was afraid to understand.

The beating of my heart, what truly could this be?
This wild, exciting feeling that came sweeping over me.

I had not known this feeling and whatever it might be.
I now cannot imagine what my world would be.

Without this precious flower I hold now in my heart,
So that now and forever more, we shall never be apart.

I saw one day, a flower that is now a part of me.
It opened up my heart and brought true love to me.

YOUR LOVE IS THE REASON

It's a crazy, aching feeling
That keeps gnawing deep inside
Affecting my every move.
I'm not able to hide
The pain on my face.
It slowly drags me down,
Swirling all around me.
I feel as if I'll drown.

Then suddenly there is sunshine
Bright, blinding light.
All the weight is lifted.
I'm now in love with life.
The reason now is clear
What caused this change I see.
Your love stands waiting,
Your arms outstretched to me.

The fog of before is lifted,
My course laid out for me.
I walk into your waiting arms
To journey forth, now free
To breathe deeply of your love.
It fills my very soul.
I must have you by my side
Before I can be whole.

I ONLY WANT

I only want a chance
    To dream the way you make me do.

I only want to feel the love
    That can only come from you.

I only want to taste life
    As it should truly be,

A life that can really happen
    With the love between you and me.

BEHIND THE POEM – LOVE'S BOUQUET

"A man falls in love with his eyes, a woman through her ears."
~Woodrow Wyatt

During our courtship, John and I spent many hours sharing our deepest thoughts, our likes and dislikes, and our secret desires.

I shared my passion for photography with John. Everywhere I went, I took my camera. I loved taking pictures of sporting events, nature and especially, children because of their thrilling spontaneity. I captured moments in time for beautiful memories.

One afternoon, I brought John two of my favorite pictures. One was a picture of a single lotus blossom in full bloom in a pond of lotus greenery. The second was a pink water lily, framed by lily pads that appeared silver due to the lighting. I loved the symbolism behind these flowers – their lovely representation of both love and life. They grow in muddy ponds and lakes, yet remain unstained, adorned in purity and beauty. I felt that I had to share these photos and their meaningful message with John.

I had placed the photos in small frames, hoping he might want to keep them. When he asked if he could have them, I gave a mental squeal of delight and gladly said yes. My heart skipped with excitement and pride as he placed them on the credenza behind his desk. A few days later, John gave me the poem **"Love's Bouquet,"** words inspired by my photos.

LOVE'S BOUQUET

Two flowers stand behind me,
From your own hand they came.
They cling so tightly together
For apart they would never be the same.

They bring a smile to my heart,
Your love grows warm within.
For they are nature's picture of you and I,
Love's bouquet 'til time does end.

OUR PATH

What might have been I do not know,
Had I sought the paths where I did not go.

Where would I be, I do not care,
For life wouldn't matter if you weren't there.

The paths I've chosen I know they're right.
When you're next to me in the dark of night.

When you hold my hand and walk next to me,
What better chance could there be.

You are my soul; you have my heart.
I pray to God that we not be apart.

For the path I walk was meant to be.
For there is only life when you are with me.

MY DEAREST GIFT TO YOU

Be gentle with my love,
It's all I have to give.
The most precious gift I own,
I offer with all my heart.

The only person who has ever
Reached so deep inside of me.
You have found worlds
I did not know existed.

Walk those worlds beside me,
Hold my heart gently,
And let me love you
For all time.

A FOREVER PROMISE

In a quiet, secluded garden,
I offered you my heart to keep and hold forever
That we might be together to share the happiness
I have only found with you.

You are all of the dreams I dared not dream . . .
All of the hopes I dared not hope . . .
All of the smiles I dared not smile.
You are the love I dared not wish for.

You have come into my life and changed it forever.
There are no thoughts in my mind that do not include you.
There is no tomorrow if you are not there.
I pray to God above, and I ask, no beg of you
To know that the love I offer is
Unconditional, undying, unchallenged, and true.

PART 2 · LIFE LOVING EACH OTHER

"Two such as you with such master speed
Cannot be parted nor be swept away
From one another once you are agreed
That life is only forevermore
Together wing-to-wing and oar-to-oar."
~Robert Frost

The greatest gift you can give to another is the gift of your time. This is perhaps the greatest lesson John and I learned from our relationship and why our love continued to grow with each passing year. Though our 19 years together went by in the blink of an eye, we lived a full life of love. We knew that it didn't necessarily matter how much time we had; it was what we did with that time together that made it count. From the first night that we lived in our little pink house, John and I were inseparable. As much as possible, we spent every waking minute together. We were best friends, constant companions, lovers, and husband and wife.

We both loved music, sports, and romantic candlelight dinners. Even our individual pastimes and hobbies soon became shared activities – cooking, hiking, gardening, and rescuing unwanted and abandoned small dogs. We nurtured our love and treated our time together as something special, whether attending music concerts and sporting events, working out together or cherishing our table-for-two dinners. We adored anything and everything that the other enjoyed because we adored one another.

Morning coffee together on a patio, balcony or sunroom was the start to our day. We could sit for hours drinking coffee and watching the birds and butterflies flit around our garden. In the springtime, we marveled as trees leafed and flowers blossomed. On clear nights, we watched the moon brighten and stars twinkle as we enjoyed an evening glass of wine.

The beach, warm sun, and John's family beckoned us to return and retire in Florida. Simple pastimes served as more reasons to enjoy time together, such as watching the sun set and listening to the waves roll onto the shore. We always thought the seagulls sounded like they were laughing at each other and at us.

John never tired of watching me delight in my passion for photography. My camera went everywhere we went, capturing photo memories of our shared experiences and passions. Yet my favorite photo subject was always my gorgeous, smiling husband.

Through poetry and photography, John and I captured the beauty that we saw in our life together. We also sought ways to add our own touches of beauty to the world. Every home we owned was a new palette for us to paint with the rich colors and textures of flowers, shrubs, and John's unique rock gardens. We added birdbaths and feeders to attract God's beautiful winged creatures. Wherever life took us, we wanted to leave a meaningful footprint of beauty.

The poems and photos that follow display the true depth of beauty that John and I saw in each other, and all around us. As you read, we want you to feel the absolute love and devotion we shared and experience how we lived life with each other – savoring the hours, minutes, and moments. Then be inspired to give the greatest gift to the ones you love – your time.

DAYBREAK

As the morning comes, and

    I find you really lying next to me,

    I am filled with a joy that

    I cannot describe.

    I am filled with love.

As the morning breaks,

    Your gentle breathing beside me

    Is the first sign that all is right with the world.

    I breathe easy knowing that you are there to love me and

    I there to love you.

As the dawn breaks,

    I watch you there next to me.

    I see your smile ease across your face, and

    I feel your warm touch and I know that

    I have found the love of my life.

NEW DAY, NEW WORLD

As the dawn
Of consciousness slowly spreads
Its light across the fields of my mind,
I find you
Gently walking there
Touching my very heart and soul,
Beckoning me to walk with you down a flower-lined path of love
To a world I have never known before.
I gladly take your hand, and
We start the day together.

YOUR SMILE

When your eyes smile at me,
The world just goes away.

I'm filled with your warm love
Beyond what words can say.

When your lips smile at me,
Great joy fills my heart.

And I know that now and forever,
We must never be apart.

WE ARE ONE

When you're in my arms and by my side,
I'm whole again and filled with pride.

When I see you there in the morning light,
I'm filled with strength; I know not fright.

When the shadows fall with the end of day,
I need you with me; it's the only way.

For you are me, and I am you,
And together we make a love that is true.

LIFE WITH YOU

To watch a flower blossom,
     to see its petals unfold,
To marvel at the magic
     I'd been too busy to behold.

To see a bird feeding,
     perched as if on a throne,
To be amazed by its beauty
     that before I had not known.

To watch the stars twinkle
     in a clear winter sky,
To wonder if there's someone there
     looking back with a questioning eye.

To sip a rich, red wine
     and feel its warm embrace,
To slow the rushing world
     to a much more reasonable pace.

To watch the fire dancing
     on a cold, winter night,
To see it sparkle in your eyes,
     as I hold you, oh, so tight.

To feel the warmth of love
     like it's never been before,
To walk with you hand-in-hand
     through life's every door.

To feel you lying next to me,

> *touching you to be sure,*

To pray you will always be there,

> *for without you, I would not endure.*

To finally live life

> *as it was surely meant to be,*

To know it would not have happened

> *if you did not love me.*

To feel the need so deep inside,

> *to say "I love you" o'er and o'er*

To pray that you will always know,

> *no one could love you more.*

WARMTH OF YOUR LOVE

You warm my heart from the chilling cold.

You warm my soul from its very depths.

You warm my smile 'til it beams with glee.

You warm all there is of me.

LOVE'S EMBERS

The fire warmly flickers.
  We nestle side by side.
    I feel like I'm drowning. I thought I'd be denied
      Knowing what true love could ever possibly be.
        Now, I'm just amazed.

The feelings inside of me explode in celebration
  Of life before unknown.
    The joy of your sweet love, the melody of your song
      Brings music to my heart that plays eternally.
        The song of two lovers, the lovers are you and me.

The fire warmly flickers;
  The flame a golden glow.
    But the warmth I feel,
      The fire will never know.

For it comes from within
  The heart and soul of me.
    From within the arms of love
      Where we shall always be.

TO MY LOVE

For all of my weaknesses, you are my strength.

For all of my failures, you are my success.

For all of my sorrows, you are my happiness.

For all that is wrong with me, you are what is right.

For all of my life, you are my love.

WE ARE LOVE

We are love, it's plain to see;
See the picture of you and me.

We are love, it's plain to see,
Read the story of you and me.

We are love, it's plain to see,
The symbol shows it's you and me.

We are love, it's plain to see,
It all points to you and me.

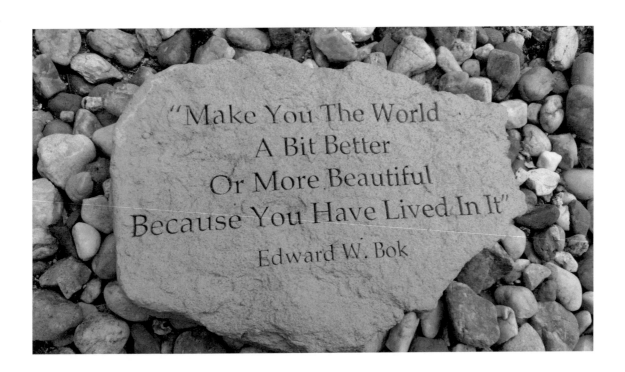

I WANT TO GROW OLD WITH YOU

I want to grow old with you

    Walking through the sands of time,

        Our footprints left side by side

            With your hand held tightly in mine.

I want to watch you grow more beautiful

    In the ways only you can do,

        And be with you every minute I can.

            I just want to grow old with you.

I want to make lots of memories

    That bring a smile as they cross your mind.

        I want to weave a spell over your heart

            That will last 'til the end of time.

I want to cherish each passing day

    And share each moment with you,

        And I want to love you forever and ever.

        I just want to grow old with you.

TRUE LOVE, FOREVER LOVE

If I could only paint a picture

    So that you would surely see

    The love I have down deep inside

    The love that has to be.

    A picture that you could look at

        And know our love is true,

        And each day you could see

        That love is me and you.

If I could only write a story

    The true tale of you and I

    That tells of the love

    That no one can deny.

    A story you can sit and read

        And know deep in your heart

        That now and forever more

        We should never be apart.

If I could only carve in stone

Somewhere for all to see

A symbol of you and I

That shows what love should be.

A carving you could look at

If doubt should come your way

That says "I will always love you

Until my dying day."

So I will paint the picture,

And the story I will tell.

In stone I'll carve the symbol,

So that you will know so well

What true love really looks like,

For it looks like you and me,

Arm-in-arm together

For all eternity.

EPILOGUE

"How do I love thee?
Let me count the ways.
I love thee with the depth and breadth and height my soul can reach . . .
I love thee with the breath, smiles and tears of all my life!
And if God choose, I shall but love thee better after death."
~Elizabeth Barrett Browning

John and I always believed that we were destined to be together, that it was part of God's plan for us. So much of our lives were guided and blessed by guardian angels – some we met and some we never met. We were blessed with a meant-to-be-moment that placed us together – forever in love, soul mates.

On June 19, 1996, John wrote "My Most Solemn Promise of Love" to me. He promised to care for me, protect me, comfort me, hold me, hug me, cherish me, kiss me, and overwhelmingly love me for the rest of his life. He promised to do his very best to make me the happiest woman in the world and love me more than anyone has been loved. For the next nineteen years, he did just that; he never reneged on his promise.

Just thirteen months after we married, John was diagnosed with lymphoma for the first time. We were devastated because we had just started our life together. He fought the cancer with all his might, and I never left his side. Through the grace of God, John enjoyed fourteen years in remission. During those years, we chose to let our memories of John's sickness enhance our time together rather than cast a fearful shadow over it. We loved each other even more intensely than before, savoring every moment and living life the only way we knew how – together. As John lovingly wrote to me, "Each moment with you is like an unexpected blessing."

In February 2015, we received the heart-wrenching news that John's cancer had recurred. It hit with such a vengeance that he was admitted to Moffitt Cancer Center and placed in ICU. Though John was very spiritual, reading the Bible and praying daily, he had never been baptized, and this became an ardent longing in his heart. On February 14, while lying in the ICU, John received his life-long desire. While we had never attended Pastor Dan's church, he came graciously in answer to my prayer and baptized John.

After five harrowing weeks at Moffitt Cancer Center, John's condition improved enough for him to come home, and we had hope. One afternoon after his return from the hospital, John expressed how sorry he was that we didn't have a romantic Valentine's Day. I told him that it was the best Valentine's Day we had ever had together, and I recounted his baptism. The look on his face was priceless. With tears streaming down his face and arms raised up toward heaven, he said, "Finally, I am a Child of the Most-high God." On Valentine's Day, John received the baptism he had always wanted. And even after our many romantic dinners, kisses, thoughtful presents, and cards, this turned out to be the greatest gift either of us could have asked for - a gift that joined our souls even more completely than before.

As John's illness progressed, we spent every moment together - holding hands, sharing kisses, and loving each other fiercely. We were given so much hope, and he battled bravely. As before, I never left his side, wanting to soak in every minute in his presence. On his last night, we renewed our wedding vows - a final sign of our eternal commitment. We always feared that we would never have enough time with each other, and we didn't. Yet through it all, we learned that love isn't time bound, and we shared a lifetime in our nineteen years together.

In one of the many cards John gave me, he wrote, "I have laughed, smiled, enjoyed, learned, adventured, experienced, held hands, cuddled, hugged, kissed, loved and lived more in the time we have been together than in my whole life." For me, this sentiment was mutual. I can honestly say I would live my lifetime with John all over again, even knowing how it would end.

This book has been a labor of love and a heart-felt mission for me - to preserve John's memory and to share his beautiful gift of writing. Most of all, though, these poems and thoughts tell our beautiful love story, one lived "arm-in-arm together for all eternity."

It is my hope that in reading our story, you have seen and felt some of the momentous beauty, joy, and love that John and I shared. More than that, though, I hope that our extraordinary gift of love will encourage you to share your heart and soul with others . . . because as my husband taught me, "True love increases as you give it away."

All profits from this book will be donated to Moffitt Cancer Center (www.moffitt.org) to support cancer research.

Printed in the United States
By Bookmasters